Macmillan/McGraw-Hill READING

Contributors

The Princeton Review, Time Magazine, Accelerated Reader

The Princeton Review is not
affiliated with Princeton
University or ETS.

learning through listening

Students with print disabilities may be eligible to obtain an accessible, audio
version of the pupil edition of this textbook. Please call Recording for the Blind &
Dyslexic at 1-800-221-4792 for complete information.

Macmillan/McGraw-Hill

A Division of The McGraw·Hill Companies

Published by Macmillan/McGraw-Hill, a division of The McGraw-Hill Companies, Inc., Two Penn Plaza, NY, NY 10121

Printed in the United States of America

ISBN 0-02-188561-3/1, Bk.1
   3 4 5 6 7 8 9 027/043 04 03 02⁻

Macmillan/McGraw-Hill READING

Authors

James Flood

Jan E. Hasbrouck

James V. Hoffman

Diane Lapp

Donna Lubcker

Angela Shelf Medearis

Scott Paris

Steven Stahl

Josefina Villamil Tinajero

Karen D. Wood

Macmillan McGraw-Hill

New York   Farmington

Day by Day

The Tickle Rhyme..6
A Poem by Ian Serraillier

Nap, Cat..8
A Phonics Rhyme

Max, the Cat 10
A Story by Ann Morris
illustrated by Kathi Ember

    Story Questions and Activities 24
    Study Skills: Book Parts: Cover, Title Page.......... 26
        LANGUAGE ARTS CONNECTION
    Test Power.. 27

The Sack..28
A Phonics Rhyme

Quack 30
A Story by Judi Barrett
illustrated by Luisa D'Augusta

    Story Questions and Activities 44
    Study Skills: Book Parts: Author and Illustrator... 46
        LANGUAGE ARTS CONNECTION
    Test Power.. 47

Jig and Tap...**48**
A Phonics Rhyme

What Does Pig Do?.........................50

A Story by Angela Shelf Medearis
illustrated by Barbara Reid

    Story Questions and Activities **64**
    Study Skills: Book Parts: Table of Contents **66**
             LANGUAGE ARTS CONNECTION
    Test Power.. **67**

Fish Dish...**68**
A Phonics Rhyme

The Path on the Map.......................70

A Social Studies Story by Jean Marzollo
illustrated by Peggy Tagel

    Story Questions and Activities **84**
    Study Skills: Book Parts: Glossary **86**
             LANGUAGE ARTS CONNECTION
    Test Power..**87**

Six Fat Pigs **88**
A Phonics Rhyme

TIME FOR KIDS

Ships...90

A Social Studies Article from the Editors of
TIME FOR KIDS

    Story Questions and Activities **98**
    Study Skills: Parts of a Magazine **100**
             LANGUAGE ARTS CONNECTION
    Test Power..**101**

A Year Later **102**
A Poem by Mary Ann Hoberman

How To **Reading a Recipe** **104**

Glossary **106**

Day by Day

The Tickle Rhyme

"Who's that tickling my back?"
said the wall.
"Me," said a small
Caterpillar. "I'm learning
To crawl."

by Ian Serraillier

Nap, Cat

Nap with a bat, cat?

Nap with a mat, cat?

Nap with a map, cat?

Nap with a cap, cat?

The best place to nap, cat,

Is to nap on my lap!

Meet Ann Morris

Ann Morris has taught in many public and private schools. She has also made several award-winning films for children. Now she spends most of her time writing children's books.

Meet Kathi Ember

Kathi Ember has two horses, three sheep, and four cats. Her pets give her ideas for her illustrations. She has illustrated children's books, greeting cards, and magazines.

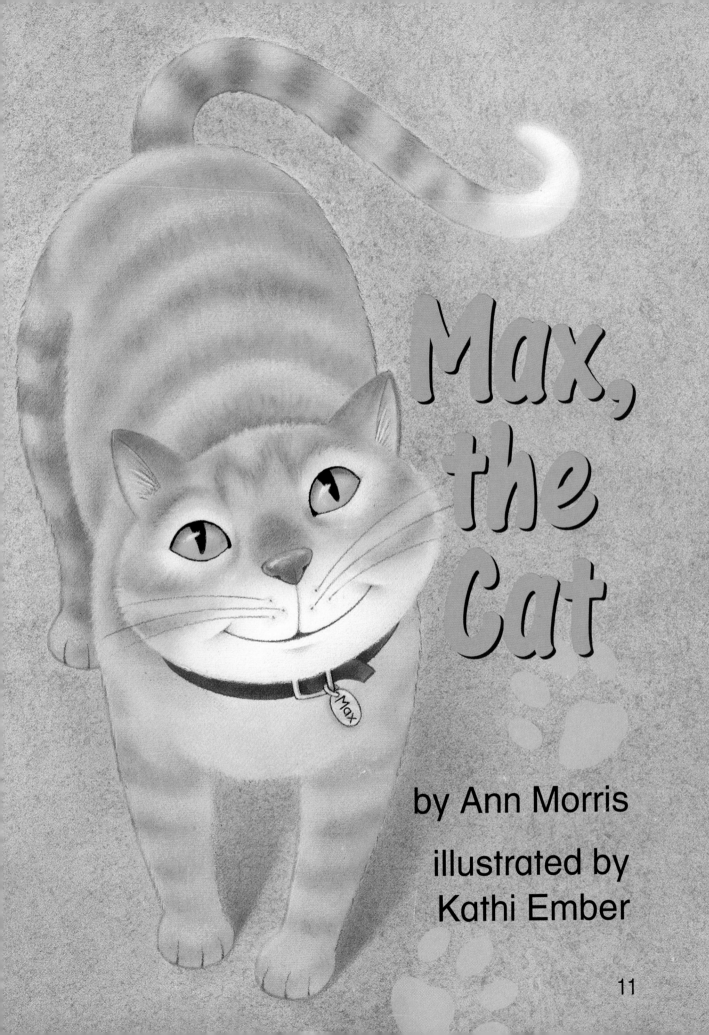

Max, the Cat

by Ann Morris

illustrated by Kathi Ember

Pam has a cat.

He is Max.

Pam has one mat.

Max likes to nap on this mat.

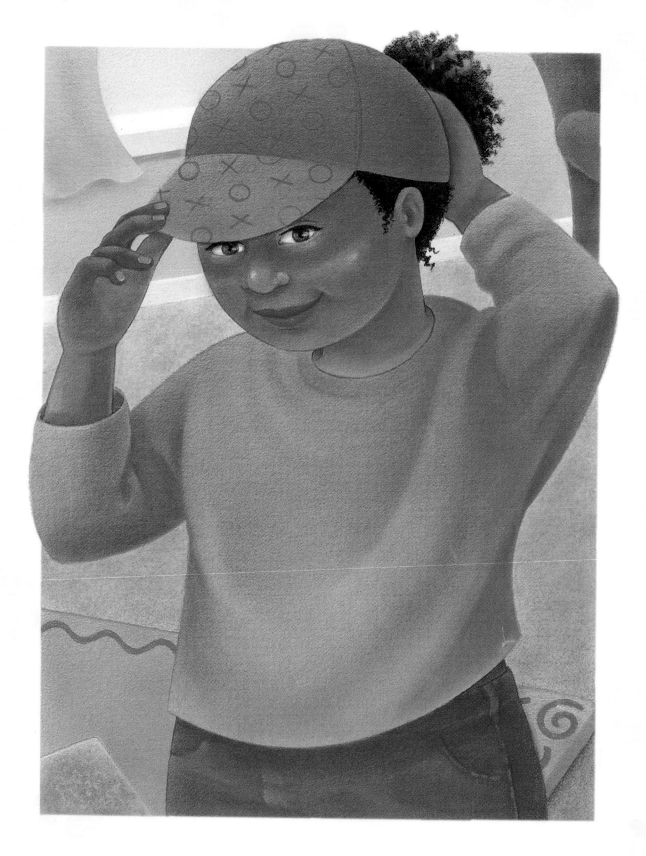

Pam has one cap.

Max likes to nap on this cap.

Pam is mad at Max.

Pam is sad.

Max is sad.

Pam gives Max a hug.

Pam gives Max a mat and a cap.

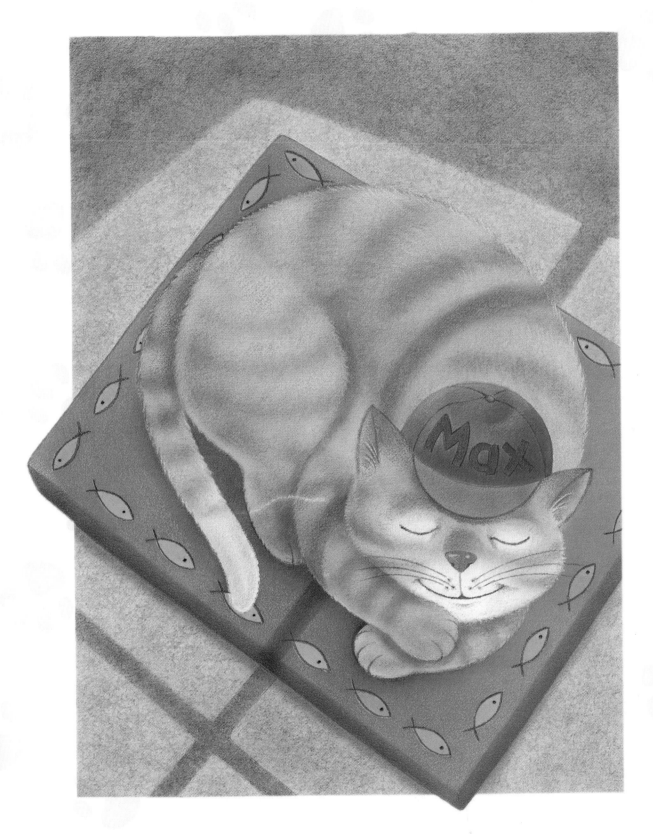

Max can nap and nap.

Story Questions & Activities

1 What does Pam have?

2 Why is Pam mad?

3 What else might Max like?

4 What is "Max, the Cat" about?

5 Is Max like a cat you read about?

Name a Cat

Draw a mat for a cat.
Write the name of the
cat on the mat.

Sam

Make a Cat

Cut shapes out of paper.
Make a cat with the shapes.
Glue the cat on paper.

Find Out More

Some cats are good pets.
Some cats are wild.
Find out about a wild cat.

Parts of a Book

Cover

title

MAMA CAT
has three kittens

Denise Fleming

picture   author

Title Page

title

Henry Holt and Company • New York

MAMA CAT
has three kittens

Denise
Fleming

author

picture

Look at the Parts of a Book

1 What is on the book cover?

2 What is on the title page?

Cat Wakes Up

Cat wakes up.

She wants food.

She will cry.

Let us feed her.

Now, she is a happy cat.

What is the title of this story?

○ The Happy Cat

○ Cat Wakes Up

The title can tell you about the story.

The Sack

Quack! Quack! Quack! Quack!

I pack a tan sack.

I pack my hat.

And I pack my bat.

I pack my ball,

And give it all to Jack.

Meet Judi Barrett

Judi Barrett has always enjoyed creating things. When she was a child, she enjoyed writing and illustrating stories. Today, she still enjoys creating the words and pictures for many children's books.

Meet Luisa D'Augusta

When Luisa D'Augusta was little, she drew many funny pictures. Today, she illustrates many children's books.

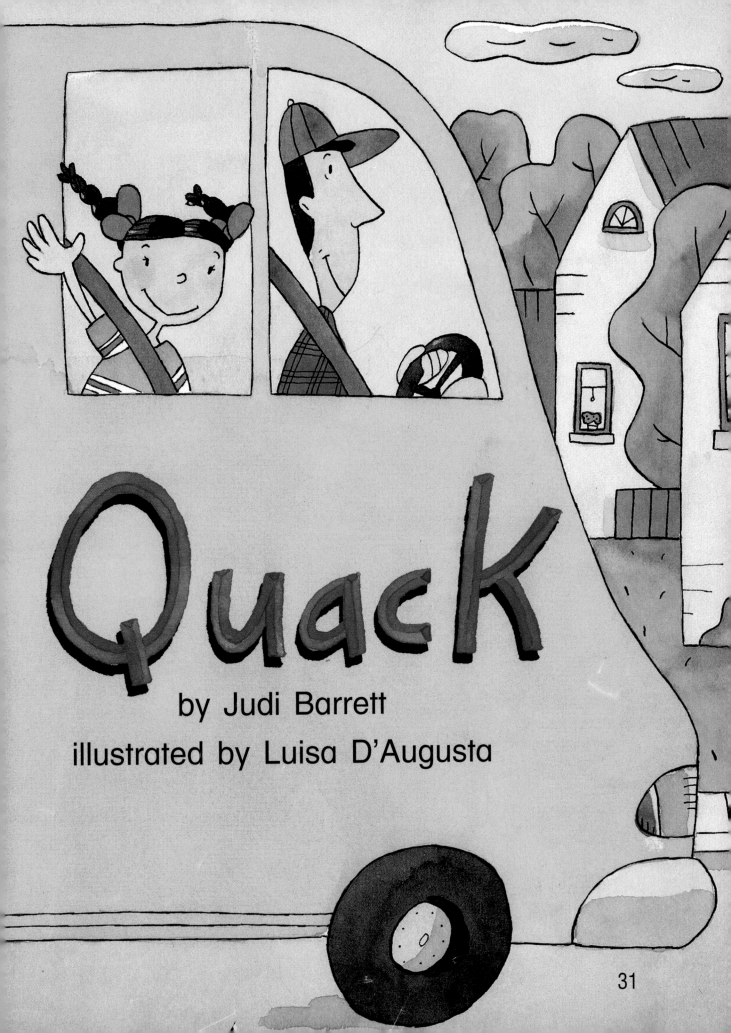

Quack

by Judi Barrett

illustrated by Luisa D'Augusta

This is Nan and Dad.

That is the tan van.

Jack and Mack help Dad.

They pack the van.

Nan packs the bat.

Nan packs the hat.

Nan packs the map.

Nan packs the cap on the bat.

"What is that Quack in back?"

"Quack can sit on your lap!"

Good-bye, Jack and Mack!

1. Who helps Dad pack?

2. Why didn't Mack and Jack get in the van?

3. Why are Dad and Nan moving?

4. Tell what Nan packed.

5. How is Quack like Max the Cat?

Make a List

Pretend you are moving.
List what you would pack.

Make a Van

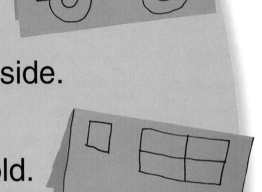

Fold a paper in half.

Draw a van on one side.

Cut the van out.

Do not cut on the fold.

Stand it up.

Find Out More

There are many kinds of ducks.

Find pictures of them.

Tell how they are alike
and different.

Parts of a Book

author

illustrator

An author writes a story.

An illustrator draws the pictures.

Sometimes the author is also the illustrator.

Look at the Book Cover

❶ Who is the author?

❷ What did the illustrator do?

On the Pond

There is a duck on the pond.

There is a frog on the pond.

The duck quacks at the frog.

The frog croaks at the duck.

The duck swims after the frog.

The frog swims away.

What is on the pond?

○ A duck

○ A swan

Sometimes pictures give clues about the story.

Jig and Tap

I see a pig in a wig.

The pig in the wig

Can dance a quick jig!

I see a pig in a cap.

The pig in the cap

Can tap and tap!

Meet Angela Shelf Medearis

Angela Shelf Medearis has loved reading books since she was a child. There were few books by or about African Americans then. Now that she is grown up, Medearis enjoys writing about African Americans.

Meet Barbara Reid

Barbara Reid has always liked to tell stories with pictures. After going to art school, she became a children's book illustrator. Many of her books have won awards.

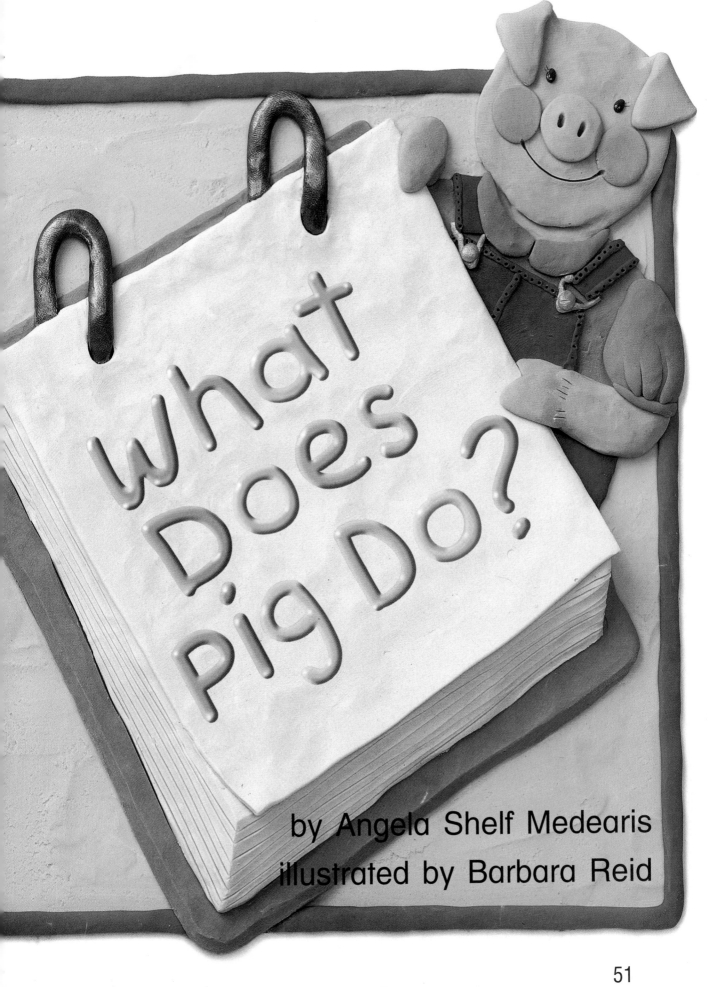

what Does Pig Do?

by Angela Shelf Medearis

illustrated by Barbara Reid

On Monday, Pig picks a wig.

Monday

On Tuesday, Pig digs and digs.

Tuesday

On Wednesday, Pig kicks and kicks.

On Thursday, Pig taps and taps.

On Friday, Pig bats and bats.

On Saturday, Pig does laps.

What does Pig do on Sunday?

Does Pig pick a wig?

Sunday
?

59

Does Pig dig and kick?

Does Pig tap and bat?

Sunday

?

Look at her there!

On Sunday, Pig naps!

Story Questions & Activities

1 What does Pig do on Friday?

2 What does Pig's calendar show?

3 Why is it good to have a calendar?

4 Act out the story.

5 In what ways are Pig and Max, the Cat the same?

Make a Calendar

Pick a day of the week.
Draw a box.
Write the day at the top.
Draw what you do on
that day.

Make a Class Book

A shovel and a pail go together.

So do a bat and a ball.

Draw two things that go together.

Make a class book.

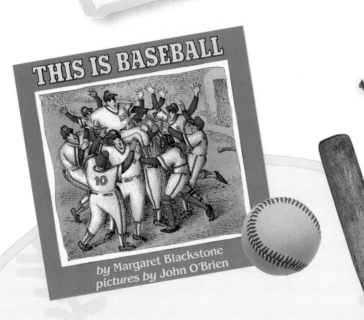

Find Out More

Choose a game or sport.

Find out how to play it.

Parts of a Book

A table of contents tells what is in a book.

It tells the page where each story begins.

CONTENTS

THE GUEST	5
STRANGE BUMPS	19
TEAR-WATER TEA	31
UPSTAIRS AND DOWNSTAIRS	41
OWL AND THE MOON	51

Look at the Table of Contents

1 What story begins on page 19?

2 Where does "The Guest" begin?

Where Was the Pig?

Pam had a pig.

It hid in the tub.

Then, it hid in the car.

Then, it hid in the bed.

Pam found her pig.

It was asleep.

Where did the pig hide first?

◯ In the tub

◯ In the bed

Read the story carefully.

Fish Dish

"I wish, wish, wish
For a dish," said the fish,
"With a yam, yam, yam,
And a little bit of jam,
And I want thin ham
With that yam!" said the fish.

Meet Jean Marzollo

Jean Marzollo likes to write children's books. She says, "It's a job, a hobby, and a game—all in one." Marzollo also likes to visit schools and talk to children about her work.

Meet Peggy Tagel

Peggy Tagel has drawn illustrations for magazines, greeting cards, and children's books. She also likes to garden and collect cookie jars.

70

THE PATH ON THE MAP

by Jean Marzollo

illustrated by Peggy Tagel

We see a path on this map.

We can go down the path.

A pig is on this map.

74

Can you see it?

A fat cow is on this map.

Can you see it?

77

A duck is on this map.

Can you see it?

79

A fish is on this map.

That is a big fish!

What could be in this shack?

82

Cats, cats, cats!

Story Questions & Activities

1 What animals are in the pond?

2 How did the map help the children?

3 What else might be in the shack?

4 Use the map to retell the story.

5 What other story has a map?

Write About a Picture

Choose one farm animal.
Write two sentences about it.

Make an Animal

Choose a farm animal.

Make the animal with clay.

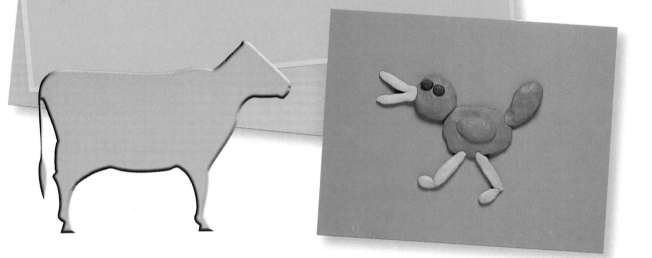

Find Out More

Look at a map of the United States.

Find your state.

Find your city.

Glossary

A Glossary is at the end of this book.

Each word in it has a picture.

The words are in ABC order.

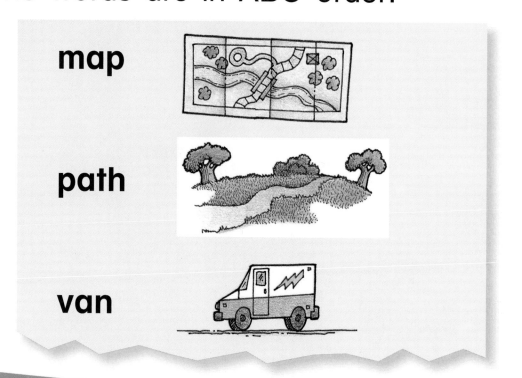

map

path

van

Look at the Glossary

1 What word comes after *map*?

2 What word shows a kind of car?

TEST POWER

Who Went to the Farm?

First, the hen went to the farm.

Then, the cow went to the farm.

Next, the lamb went to the farm.

Last, the boy went to the farm.

Then, the farm was full.

Who went to the farm last?

○ The lamb

○ The boy

Read the question carefully before you answer it.

Six Fat Pigs

Six fat pigs on a ship,

Dip,

　Dip,

　　Dip for fish.

A fish for duck, and one for cat,

And the pigs can have their wish.

TIME
FOR KIDS

Ships

Look at the big ship.

It has sails.

This one is a steam ship.

Look at this ship.

It is a Navy ship.

What ship is that?

A story from the editors of *TIME FOR KIDS*.

This one is my ship!

1. What did the first ship have?

2. What helps a big ship move?

3. When is it better to use a ship than a truck?

4. Name ships you read about.

5. What other story in this unit shows a way of getting places?

Write a Log

Pretend you are on a ship.
Write about what happens.

Monday: October 4, 2002
We had to fix a sail.

Make a Raft

Use heavy cardboard.

Draw a raft shape on it.

Cut out the raft.

Make a notch in the back.

Put a bit of soap in the notch.

See if the raft floats in water.

Find Out More

Find out one new thing about ships.

Write a sentence.

Draw a picture and name your ship.

STUDY SKILLS

Parts of a Magazine

Look at the Magazine Cover

1 What is the name of the magazine?

2 What pictures are on the cover?

Get Up

Get up Sun.

It is day.

Rise up in the sky.

Shine all day.

Shine on the ships on the sea.

Shine on the shells on the beach.

Shine on you.

Shine on me.

In this story,

the sun shines on —

○ the hills

○ the ships

> **Look for the answer that fits the story.**

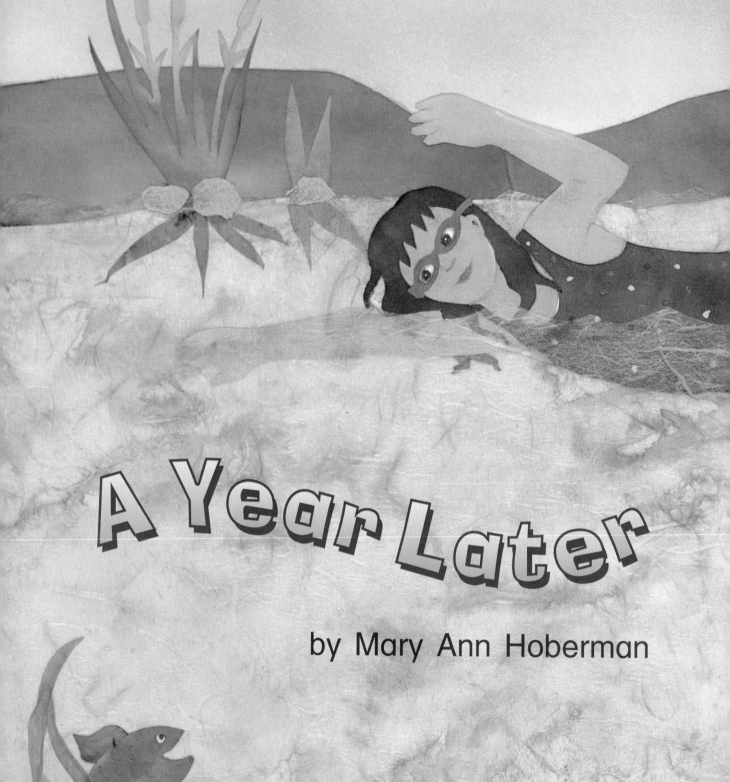

A Year Later

by Mary Ann Hoberman

Last summer I couldn't swim at all;

I couldn't even float;

I had to use a rubber tube

Or hang on to a boat;

I had to sit on shore

While everybody swam;

But now it's this summer

And I can!

Reading a Recipe

A recipe tells you how to make something step by step. You can follow a recipe to make lemonade.

Lemonade

You will need:

2 lemons

1 cup of water

3 spoons of sugar

Follow these steps:

1. First, squeeze the lemons.

2. Next, mix the lemon juice and water.

3. Last, add the sugar and stir.

Questions

1 What do you do first?

2 What do you do last?

Glossary

This glossary can help you to find out the meanings of words in this book that you may not know.

The words are listed in alphabetical order. There is a picture and a simple sentence for each word. You can use the picture and sentence to help you understand the meaning of each word.

Sample Entry

Main Entry　　**Sample Sentence**

Mat

The cat is sleeping on its **mat.**

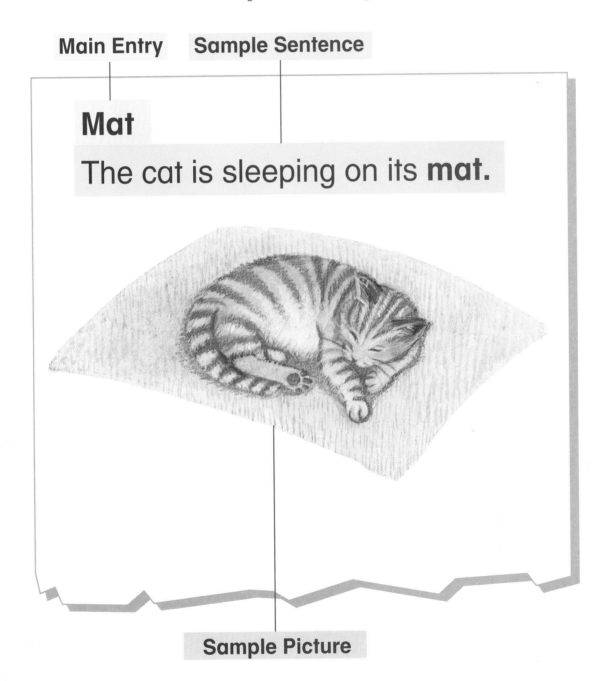

Sample Picture

Bat

Jim hits the ball with a **bat.**

Big

Our beach ball is **big.**

Cap

Zack wears his team's **cap.**

Cow

A **cow** is a farm animal that gives milk.

Dig

Nick uses a shovel to **dig.**

Fish

Fish live in the water.

Hat

Farmer Tad is wearing a **hat** on his head.

Hug

Cal gets a **hug** from Mom.

Map

A **map** shows where places are.

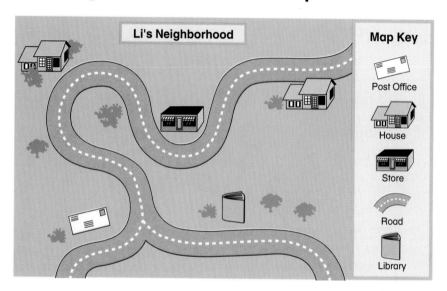

Mat

The cat is sleeping on its **mat.**

Path

A clear **path** makes it easier to get into your home.

Sails

The **sails** help the boats move.

Ship

A **ship** is a big boat.

Steam

The **steam** is coming out of the ship's stack.

Van

We ride a **van** to school.

Wig

A **wig** can be fun to wear.

ACKNOWLEDGMENTS

The publisher gratefully acknowledges permission to reprint the following copyrighted material:

"The Tickle Rhyme" by Ian Serraillier. Reprinted by permission.

"A Year Later" from THE LLAMA WHO HAD NO PAJAMA: 100 FAVORITE POEMS. Copyright 1959 and renewed 1987 by Mary Ann Hoberman. Reprinted by permission of Harcourt, Inc.

Illustration
Jack Graham, 6-7; Mircea Catusanu, 8-9; Kathi Ember, 10-23, 24tl; Daniel Del Valle, 24br, 25tr, 45tr, 69cr, 85; Ken Bowser, 27, 87; Michele Noiset, 28-29; Luisa D'Augusta, 30-43, 44tl; Doug Roy, 44b, 86; Bernard Adnet, 47br, 101br; Mas Miyamoto, 47tr, 101tr; Darcia Labrosse, 48-49; Barbara Reid, 50-64; Eldon Doty, 67; Don Sullivan, 68-69; Peggy Tagel, 70-83; Jennifer Rarey, 88-89; Cecily Lang, 102-103; Felipe Galindo, 108, 110; Holly Jones, 109, 112; Peter Fasolino, 111, 115.

Photography
All photographs are by the McGraw-Hill School Division, except as noted below:

5: b. Ulrike Welsch/Photo Researchers. 10: b. Courtesy of H.K. Portfolio Inc.; t. courtesy of Ann Morris. 25: PhotoDisc. 30: b. Courtesy of Luisa D'Augusta; t. Courtesy of Judi Barrett. 45: PhotoDisc. 45: bc PhotoDisc. 45: br PhotoDisc. 50: b. © Ian Crysler '97/Noodle Studio; t. Diva Productions, Inc. 65: PhotoDisc. 70: b.l. Jim Foster/The Stock Market; c.l. Courtesy of H.K. Portfolio Inc.; r. Index Stock Photography; t.l. Ellen Warner. 71: b. Gary Landsman/The Stock Market. 75: b. Index Stock Photography. 77: b. Index Stock Photography. 79: Gary Landsman/The Stock Market. 81: b. National Audubon Society/Photo Researchers, Inc. 83: b. Larry West/FPG International; t. American Images/FPG International. 84: l. Index Stock Photography; t.r. National Audubon/Photo Researchers, Inc.; c.r. Jim Foster/The Stock Market; b.r. Kathi Lamm/Stone. 106: PhotoDisc. 109: b. Renee Lynn/Stone/PNI. 111: Paul Chesley/Stone. 113: b. Jim Brown/The Stock Market; t. Gay Bumgarner/Stone. 114: b. Nancy Simmermanz/Allstock/PNI; t. Ray Soto/The Stock Market. 115: Douglas Peebles/Words & Pictures/PNI.

READING FOR INFORMATION
All illustrations and photographs are by Macmillan/McGraw-Hill (MMH) except as noted below:
Photography
104: Ken Karp for MMH. 105: Dave Mager for MMH.

Illustration
104–105: Susan Synarski.